In The Wild

Crocodiles

Claire Robinson

Produced by Times, Malaysia
Designed by Celia Floyd
Cover design by Lucy Smith

01 00 99 98 97
10 9 8 7 6 5 4 3 2 1

ISBN 1-57572-133-3

Library of Congress Cataloging-in-Publication Data

Robinson, Claire, 1955-
    Crocodiles / Claire Robinson.
       p.   cm. -- (In the wild)
    Includes bibliographical references (p.   ) and index.
    Summary: Looks at the daily lives of crocodiles, describing where
they live, how thy hunt, how they care for their young, and more.
    ISBN 1-57572-133-3 (lib. bdg.)
    1. Crocodiles--Juvenile literature.   [1. Crocodiles.]   I. Title.
II. Series: Robinson, Claire, 1955-   In the wild.
QL666.P925R635 1997
597. 98--dc21

                                     97-12300
                                       CIP
                                       AC

Acknowledgements

The author and publishers are grateful to the following for permission to reproduce copyright
photographs:
Ardea London Ltd, Werner Curth p.4 bottom, Ferrero-Labat p.8, ME England p.9,
Reg Morrison p.23; BBC Natural History Unit, Ron O'Connor p.10; FLPA, p.22;
NHPA, A.N.T. p.15, Mandal Ranjit p.5 top, Steve Robinson p.5 bottom, Kevin Schafer p.21;
Oxford Scientific Films, Terry Button p.12, Mark Deeble & Victoria Stone pp.13, 14, 17, 18, 19,
20, Carol Farneti p.6, Belinda Wright pp.11, 16, Claire Robinson, p.7.

Cover photograph: Oxford Scientific Films

Special thanks to Oxford Scientific Films

Every effort has been made to contact copyright holders of any material reproduced in this
book. Any omissions will be rectified in subsequent printings if notice is given to the publisher.

Some words are shown in bold, **like this**. You can find out what they mean by looking in
the glossary.

Contents

Crocodile Relatives

Crocodiles are a type of **crocodilian**. There are 22 kinds of crocodilian. Here you can see some of them. An alligator is also a kind of crocodilian.

caiman

alligator

gharial

crocodile

When a crocodile closes its mouth, you can still see some of its teeth.

What's it like to be a crocodile?

Where Crocodiles Live

Crocodiles live in rivers and lakes. They live in hot parts of Africa, Asia, North and South America, and Australia.

These crocodiles live near the **Nile** River.
They are warming themselves in the sun.
They don't mind sharing the riverbank,
but they spend a lot of time alone.

Moving Around

Crocodiles swim by sweeping their strong, **scaly** tails from side to side.

On land their short legs can move quite fast, but they don't often run. They may run to water for safety if they are scared.

Basking

Crocodiles are **reptiles**. They cannot keep warm like we can. They need to **bask** in the sun every morning to warm up.

Sometimes they bask with their mouths open. All their teeth are the same shape. Look how sharp they are!

Hunting

Crocodiles hunt animals for food. This crocodile is out hunting. Only its eyes, ears, and **nostrils** show above the water. Other animals will not see it coming.

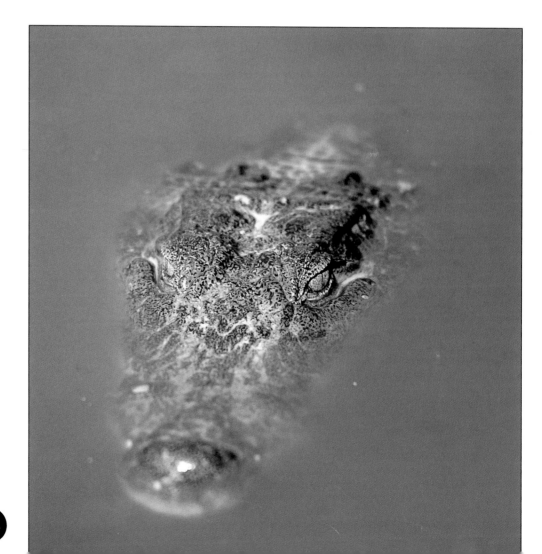

Some **wildebeest** have come to drink
from the river. The crocodile leaps
forward to catch one. The frightened
animals are lucky. They get away.

Eating

This time the crocodile is lucky. As a **wildebeest** crosses the river, it lunges forward with its jaws open.

The crocodile drags the wildebeest to the
bottom of the river to eat. After eating,
it rests.

Babies

Once a year, female crocodiles dig nests to lay their eggs in. They do this during the night. This female has covered her nest with leaves.

Many weeks later, the baby crocodiles begin to hatch from their shells. Their mother hears them calling and helps to dig them out of the nest.

Growing Up

Baby crocodiles must quickly learn how to survive. **Basking** in the sun is very important. This seven-week-old baby is basking on her mother's foot.

The young crocodile must learn to hunt.
It cannot chew, so it looks for food that it
can swallow whole. This dragonfly
looks tasty!

Danger!

There is danger in the river for young crocodiles. This baby is being eaten by a huge fish called a Nile perch.

Adult crocodiles are in danger too. People kill them, as well as other **reptiles**, for their **scaly** skin. It is turned into leather for bags, belts, and shoes.

Crocodile Facts

- Crocodiles hunt **mammals**, birds, and fish for food. They can eat under water. After a big meal, they may not need food for a few days, or even months.

- Crocodiles cannot chew. They tear their food and swallow big pieces. They often lose teeth, but these grow back.

- Crocodiles can be very noisy. They call, roar, hiss, and **bellow** at each other.

- The world's largest **reptile** is the saltwater crocodile. It can be over 19 feet long. It lives in parts of Asia and northern Australia.

saltwater crocodile

Glossary

bask   Lie in the sun and warm up.

bellow   Call in a loud, deep voice.

crocodilians   Reptiles with the same shape as crocodiles.

mammals   Animals that feed their babies on milk, like us.

Nile   Long river in Africa.

nostrils   Holes in your nose that you breathe through.

reptiles   Animals that have hard, dry scales and need to bask in the sun to keep their bodies warm.

scaly   Skin that has scales is scaly. Scales are a skin covering.

wildebeest   Hoofed animal with horns.

Index

More Books To Read

Barrett, Norman S. *Crocodiles and Alligators.* Danbury, Conn.: Watts, 1990.

Hogan, Paula Z. *The Crocodile.* Austin, Tex.: Raintree Steck-Vaughn, 1979.

Stone, Lynn. *Crocodiles.* Vero Beach, Fla.: Rourke, 1990.